Bill Caldwell

CARTOONS

DAILY Star

AN EXPRESS BOOKS PUBLICATION

£2.50

THE DOG WRITES...

Dear Reader, bet you're surprised to see I can ~~not~~ write! Well we're not all ~~useless with a pen~~ useless with a pen and I often leave notes for my "master". I tell him what I think about what's going on in the world and where I want him to put me in the ~~~~ cartoon every day. And sometimes he gives me a tin of dog food (I have to open it myself) Thank you for following me AND HIM in the Daily Star every day. We both hope you enjoy ~~like~~ our book. I Must away now - it's time for my walk.

MR. Spot

"Same here — it's all we can afford"

(Headline: Mortgage rate goes up and up.)

. . . "And he'll chalk his cue 635 times"

January 25, 1989

"Can you help me find a seat?"

(Headline: Guardian Angels from U.S.A. patrol tube.)

"Then right after it finished he suggested we watch it all again on video."

"I don't think that's quite what she meant, Brucie."

"We have become a grandson"

May 9, 1989

(Headline: Proposals for streamlining Social Security payments.)

"Aren't we supposed to protect the PASSENGERS?"

(Headline: Guardian Angels start tube patrols during Tube drivers strike.)   *May 16, 1989*

May 17, 1989   *(Headline: Robert Swan completes walk to North Pole.)*

And anyway . . . who needs a Channel Tunnel?

May 18, 1989

13

"How's married life? — Not so hot . . . Bill's got me ironing every night."

(Headline: Bill Wyman marries Mandy Smith.)

"More coffee, dear? Oh look — it's that lovely romantic commercial"

"Are you SURE this is Majorca?"

June 9, 1989   (Headline: Air traffic delays and re-routings at time of unrest in China.)

"*TERRIBLE* expense, dear — I've had to put all my girls up in a hotel"

June 22, 1989

"I KNOW it's probably quicker, Diana — but people expect you to arrive in a limo"

June 29, 1989

"What fun Victoria — we'll be able to shop together"

July 12, 1989

19

"It's worse than we thought — they're not railmen, they're commuters."

July 14, 1989

"They're on HALVES now, but they won't last long in this heat."

July 20, 1989

21

July 21, 1989

I wonder if you'd mind crying into this bucket sir, your ex-ministerial car needs a wash

July 24, 1989

"Well? Don't you WANT to save water?"

"Very nice — who is it?"

"Do you think the Government sex survey would have been: Intrusive? Fairly Intrusive? Very Intrusive?"

September 11, 1989

"Welcome fellow Democrats, Social Democrats, Social Liberal Democrats, Liberal Social Democrats, Liberals . . ."

(Headline: Party Conference time.)

September 12, 1989

"And then in Part 2 of my book Budgie will lay an egg . . .

"It's something to do with our policy of reducing the population"

September 20, 1989

"It would be cheaper to give the ambulancemen the money"

September 22, 1989

"So YOU'RE the SDP — I thought it was going to be some sort of conference"

(Headline: Annual SDP Conference.)　　　　　　　*September 25, 1989*

"Now, you might ask 'how can you tell the drug people from the rest?'"

September 29, 1989   *(Headline: British forces co-operate in Colombian drug war.)*

"Hear that? TOLD YOU they'd be shouting for me"

(Headline: Annual Tory Party Conference.)   *October 12, 1989*

October 30, 1989   *(Headline: Lawson resigns.)*

(Headline: Kylie Minogue popularity poll.)

October 31, 1989

"Stand aside please — let 'em through, there's going to be an accident"

November 1, 1989

"And if you want the horse to go FASTER . . ."

(Headline: Court hears of laser beam binoculars designed to knock out horse race favourites.)

November 2, 1989

"Careful with him — he hurt his back picking up an 11 per cent pay rise"

November 6, 1989

"Name, rank, number and what action were you involved in?"

(Headline: Army called out during ambulance strike.)   *November 8, 1989*

39

"Mein Gott! Don't you watch television?"

November 10, 1989

"Frieda's waited YEARS for a nice rockery"

(Headline: Berlin wall comes down.)   *November 13, 1989*

"Yes, we're hoping to make a bit when it goes private"

November 23, 1989   *(Headline: Water shares price announced.)*

"It's the biggest ballooning challenge ever — getting that thing back in the box!"

(Headline: Richard Branson's Trans-Pacific balloon trip called off.)   *November 27, 1989*

"Didn't he used to be called Paul McCartney?"

November 29, 1989   *(Headline: Paul McCartney announces multi-million pound sponsorship
of his world tour by "Visa".)*

"You're not off a boat, are you?"

(Headline: Vietnamese boat people turned away from Hong Kong.)   December 14, 1989

"Gone at £160,000 . . . plus £50 for the Lada that goes with it"

"Mr Lee van Cleef? Sure you wouldn't be happier in the *other* place?"

December 18, 1989

December 20, 1989

"Wow! Looks like a White Christmas after all, Sir!"

(Headline: U.S. troops operation in Noriega's Panama.)　　　*December 21, 1989*

"Never could spell the bastard's name"

December 28, 1989

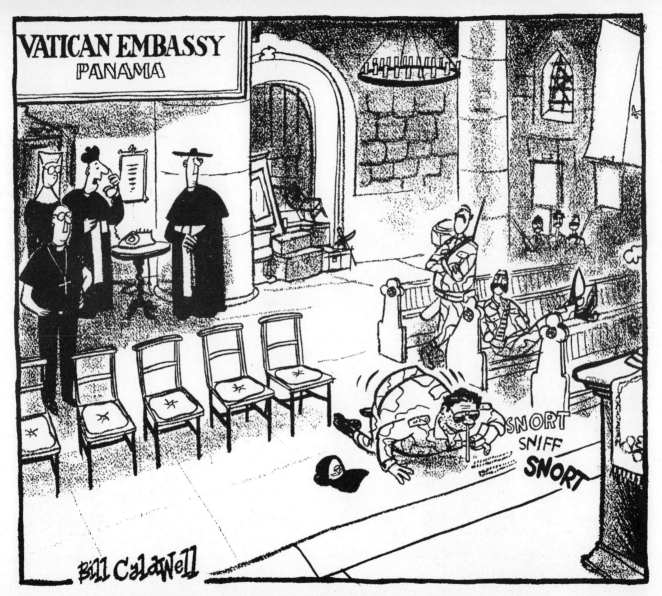

"Noriega seems very religious — he's spending a lot of time on his knees"

(Headline: Noriega seeks refuge in Vatican Embassy.)   *December 29, 1989*

"DO change your underwear, Kenneth — you never know when you'll have an accident."

"Get anything in the Harrods sale, dear?"

"THAT'S HIM! THAT'S NORIEGA."

"Bastards! They're shooting to kill"

January 16, 1990

"The new gun works pretty well, Sir — as long as you THROW IT at the target."

January 18, 1990   (Headline: Army criticism of new SA80 rifle.)

"I don't wish to be morbid — but I hear they're splitting EVERYTHING down the middle."

(Headline: Princess Anne and Mark Phillips to separate.) *January 23, 1990*

January 24, 1990

"Well, I suppose it's all right — as long as you walk three paces behind me"

(Headline: Diana visits mosque, covers her head with scarf.)   *January 25, 1990*

59

"That looks like ours . . ."

(Headline: Winter storms hit the U.K.)

"Well, it's one way of going all-seater — bring your own"

(Headline: Football clubs urged to become "all seater" arenas.)

January 31, 1990

February 2, 1990 (Headline: McDonald's open up in Moscow.)

"Er . . . just clock in like everybody else, Mr Lawson"

(Headline: Nigel Lawson gets highly-paid job at Barclays Bank.)   *February 5, 1990*

"Not now, 'Arry — know what I mean?"

February 6, 1990   *(Headline: Frank Bruno gets married.)*

"D'you mind if me and Suzie skip the campfire stuff and go for an early night?"

(Headline: Girls allowed to join Scouts.)

February 9, 1990

65

"I haven't started counting yet"

February 12, 1990   *(Headline: Nelson Mandela released.)*

"What's the matter, Mr Harris — you no like your dish on fire?"

(Headline: Richard Harris escapes small fire at Savoy Hotel.)   *February 13, 1990*

"We've attracted a whole new range of customers since we stopped doing furs"

(Headline: Harrods ban real furs.)

"EAU NO!"

(Headline: Perrier water found to contain unacceptable levels of benzine.)   *February 16, 1990*

69

"Well, we've still got our socks"

February 21, 1990   (Headline: Receivers called in to Sock Shop.)

70

"Won't be long now — it's almost settled"

(Headline: Ambulance strike nears the end.)　　　　　*February 22, 1990*

February 23, 1990

"It's as good a way to settle damages as any."

(Headline: Tessa Sanderson libel suit settled.)

March 2, 1990

73

"Maggie's right, of course . . . the poll tax is the fairest system"

"... AND we're saving about £2,000 a year on poll tax"

March 9, 1990

March 12, 1990   *(Headline: Rumour of Tory M.P.s fed up with Maggie Thatcher.)*

"And what about the weather, I hear you ask . . ."

(Headline: Manchester bids for 1996 Olympics.)

March 15, 1990

"Poor Sisters of Clare? Never heard of them"

March 22, 1990

(Headline: Belgian Nuns run off to the South of France with their funds.)

"Naturally, we're all very saddened that you've decided to leave, Dr Runcie"

(Headline: Archbishop of Canterbury announces retirement.)   *March 26, 1990*

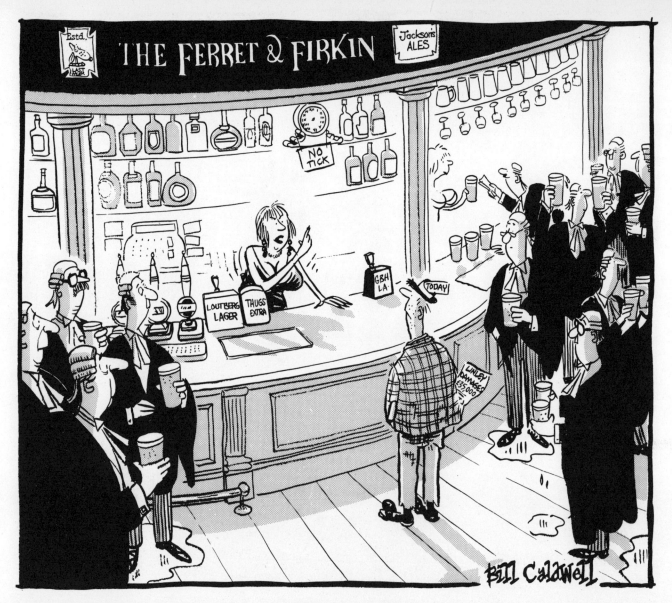

"I TOLD you — no tick"

March 30, 1990   *(Headline: Ferret & Firkin barmaid's story causes "Today" to pay £35,000*
libel damages to Lord Linley.)

"Last time the earth moved for me was 1929"

(Headline: Earthquake hits Britain.)

April 4, 1990

"Er, when you've FINISHED telling them about the Four-in-a-Bed Trial . . ."

April 5, 1990   *(Headline: Prince Philip visits High Court and hears evidence in "spicy" case.)*

"What's all the fuss about — who's going to notice another 50,000?"

(Headline: Hurd announces 50,000 Hong Kong citizens allowed into Britain.)   *April 6, 1990*

"Excuse me, but I think you've got the wrong idea about this"

April 10, 1990

"Right . . . you can be Manchester United and we'll be Oldham"

(Headline: Manchester United and Oldham reach semi-final of Cup Final; Princess Diana's family party fly to the Virgin Islands.)

April 11, 1990

"Come, come, Your Honour — you're saying NO but you really mean YES"

April 12, 1990   *(Headline: Judge says woman who said "No" to rape really meant "Yes".)*

"Parasols . . . beach beds . . . bullet-proof vests . . ."

(Headline: Great train robber Charlie Wilson shot at his home on Costa del Sol.)   *April 25, 1990*

April 27, 1990   (Headline: Home Secretary Waddington blamed for roof protests by inmates
at various prisons around the country.)

"There's nothing on"

May 1, 1990

"You're right — May Day isn't what it used to be"

May 2, 1990

"No, we're 071 actually."

(Headline: New London telephone codes introduced.)   *May 7, 1990*

"Well, HE looks harmless enough."

May 8, 1990   *(Headline: Moynihan has talks with Italians over security for World Cup.)*

"Of course it's a very, very long time since we had Royalty here in Hungary"

May 9, 1990

93

May 11, 1990   *(Headline: Big "Daily Star" story on animal cruelty and gin-traps.)*

"I'm on your side — HONEST!"

(Headline: Rumour of Heseltine challenging Maggie for leadership of the Tory Party.)   *May 14, 1990*

"I don't think that's funny"

May 15, 1990 *(Headline: "Mad Cow" disease hits the news.)*

"Quick! Fall over and roll your eyes"

(Headline: "Mad Cow" disease sweeps the country — many switch to pork or lamb.)   *May 17, 1990*

"Hello Control — yes, we're really worried — can't wait to get back home."

May 21, 1990 *(Headline: Soviet cosmonauts stuck in space.)*

"Mermen? We've been at sea too long, girls"

(Headline: All-girl crew of "Maiden" finish Round-the-World Yacht Race.)　　　*May 23, 1990*

"It's such a long time since we rolled out the carpet for Royalty . . . OOPS!"

May 25, 1990   *(Headline: Princess Royal visits Russia.)*

"Well, REALLY!"

(Headline: Introduction of new £5 note.)

June 6, 1990

June 7, 1990

(Headline: Football fans deported from Sardinia.)

"Don't worry . . . this is perfectly normal for an overpaid spoilt brat from New York"

(Headline: McEnroe back at Wimbledon.)　　　　　　　　　　　*June 8, 1990*

"Wonderful! See how he smiles and nods his head as he listens to a translation of your speech."

June 11, 1990   *(Headline: Russia at the World Cup.)*

"Please! Please tell us who won — SOB — we'll never be naughty hooligans again!"

(Headline: English football hooligans jailed.) *June 12, 1990*

105

"All change for London and the North"

June 14, 1990

"What's alla the fuss about? They don't wanna score anyhow!"

(Headline: Bad results for England in World Cup; rumours of "hanky panky" with hotel receptionist.) June 15, 1990

June 18, 1990 *(Headline: The Queen asks Maggie Thatcher to find proper jobs for younger Royals.)*

"How awful! Did you know one of those dreadful football hooligans nearly became an MP?"

(Headline: English football "hooligan" discovered to have been a Labour Candidate.)   *June 20, 1990*

"Are you QUITE sure you're ready to branch out on your own, Edward?"

June 21, 1990   (Headline: Prince Edward quits Andrew Lloyd-Webber's Really Useful Company to go on his own.)

"Excuse me, where are the ECUs?"

(Headline: Talk of Britain dropping pounds and going over to European Currency Units.)   *June 22, 1990*

July 3, 1990 (Headline: Prince Charles breaks his arm whilst playing polo.)

"Please don't get so excited, Mein Fuhrer — it's only a game of football."

"All the agents have been on and we've got a great sponsorship offer"

July 6, 1990

"Did you get his registration number?"

(Headline: Lords vote on dog registration.)

July 9, 1990

"No it's not Paul Gascoigne — this is ME!"

July 10, 1990　　　*(Headline: Gascoigne wears falsies on England team's triumphant homecoming.)*

"Not many people escape INTO Albania Mr Scargill"

(Headline: Albania: last Communist country to let its' people out.
Arthur Scargill on defensive over miners' funds.)

July 11, 1990

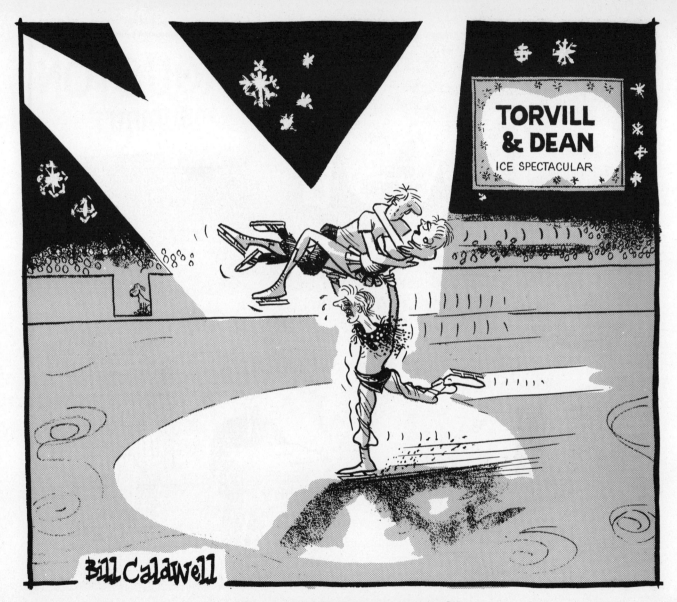

"Do you think he suspects anything?"

July 12, 1990 *(Headline: Jayne Torvill announces her marriage plans.)*

"So much for our whip-round, Helmut"

July 13, 1990

119

July 17, 1990 *(Headline: Neil Kinnock visits U.S.A. whilst British Press talk of nothing else but Nicholas Ridley's "Hitler" blunders.)*

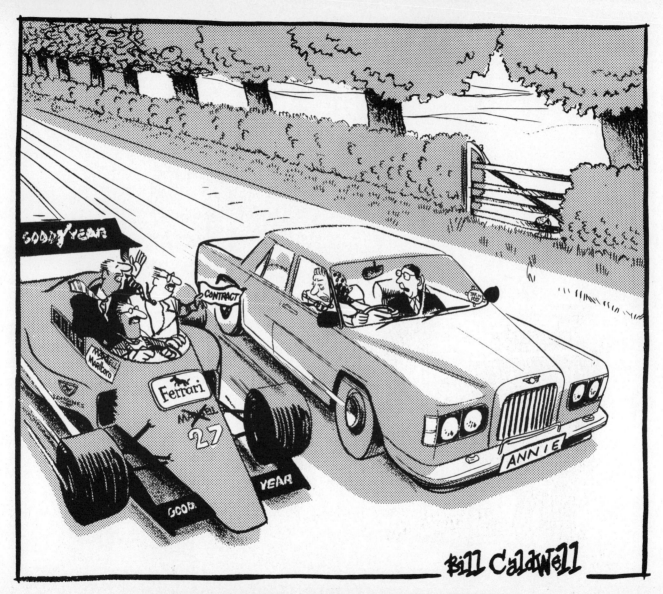

"It's not the police Ma'am, it's Ferrari — they need a new driver"

(Headline: Princess Anne does a ton: Nigel Mansell sensationally quits Ferrari Racing Team.)   *July 18, 1990*

121

I don't remember anyone coming round . . .

"Now . . . don't be frightened. It's just Madonna and her nice minders."

July 20, 1990

123

"Sorry, no . . . nothing yet!"

July 23, 1990   *(Headline: Reduction in numbers of armed forces.)*

"I'm saving LOTS of water — you're the third friend I've shared with this week"

July 24, 1990

125

"There now — that's MUCH better, isn't it?"

(Headline: Maggie Thatcher's re-shuffle of Junior Ministers.)

"Well, I'm SORRY — but I'm not very good left-handed"

July 26, 1990

"And a special mention for St Coral, St Ladbroke and St William Hill, without whose help we could not have built the new roof . . . the underground car park . . . the jacuzzi . . ."

July 27, 1990
(Headline: New Archbishop of Canterbury tip-off – betting shops cleaned out.)

128